ALL TIME FAVORITE
VIOLIN SOLOS

Ed. 3476

ISBN 978-0-7935-4804-0

G. SCHIRMER, Inc.

DISTRIBUTED BY

HAL•LEONARD®
CORPORATION

7777 W. BLUEMOUND RD. P.O. BOX 13819 MILWAUKEE, WI 53213

CONTENTS

Aurore
Aurora

Arranged by Arthur Hartmann

Gabriel Fauré

48615cx

Serenade

Edited by P. Mittell

Joseph Haydn

L'Abeille
(The Bee)

Edited by P. Mittell

François Schubert

Le Cygne
(The Swan)
from The Carnival of Animals

Edited by P. Mittell

Camille Saint-Saëns

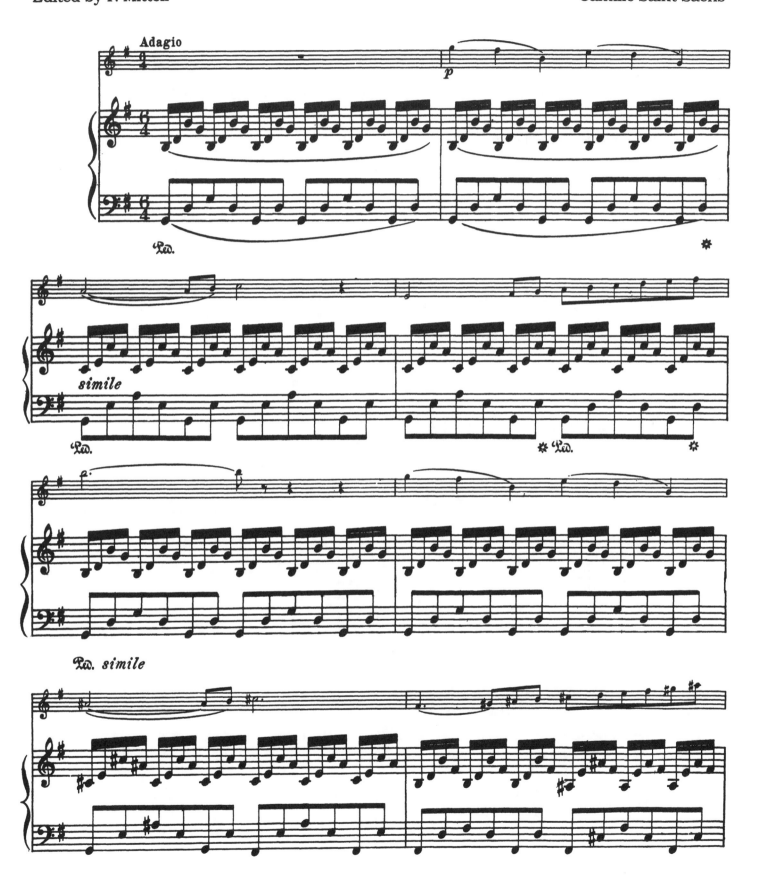

Largo
from Xerxes

Edited by P. Mittell

George Frideric Handel

Canzonetta
from Violin Concerto

Peter Ilyitch Tchaikovsky, Op. 35

Barcarolle
(Belle Nuit)
from The Tales of Hoffmann

Transcribed by A.W. Lilienthal

Jacques Offenbach

Serenata

Transcribed by F. Rehfeld

Moritz Moszkowski, Op. 15, No. 1

Hejre Kati
Scene from the Czárda

Edited by P. Mittell

Jenö Hubay, Op. 32, No. 4

Allegro moderato (♩=100)

Träume
(Dreams)

Edited by P. Mittell

Richard Wagner

Walther's Prize-Song
from Die Meistersinger

Edited by P. Mittell

Paraphrase by August Wilhelmj

42

48615

Kol Nidrei
Hebrew Melody

Edited by P. Mittell

Max Bruch, Op. 47

Adagio, ma non troppo

Romance
from Second Concerto

Edited by P. Mittell

Henri Wieniawski, Op. 22

Andante non troppo

Air

Arranged by August Wilhelmj

Johann Sebastian Bach

Beau Soir

Arranged by Arthur Hartmann

Claude Debussy

Andante, ma non troppo

One pedal to each measure

Menuet
from Quintet in E

Arranged by F. Hermann

Edited by P. Mittell

Luigi Boccherini

Wiegenlied
(Cradle Song)

Arranged by F. Hermann
Revised by P. Mittell

Johannes Brahms, Op. 49, No. 4

Dolce con moto

Rêverie
Adagio for Violin and Piano

Edited by Henry Schradieck

Henri Vieuxtemps, Op. 22, No. 3

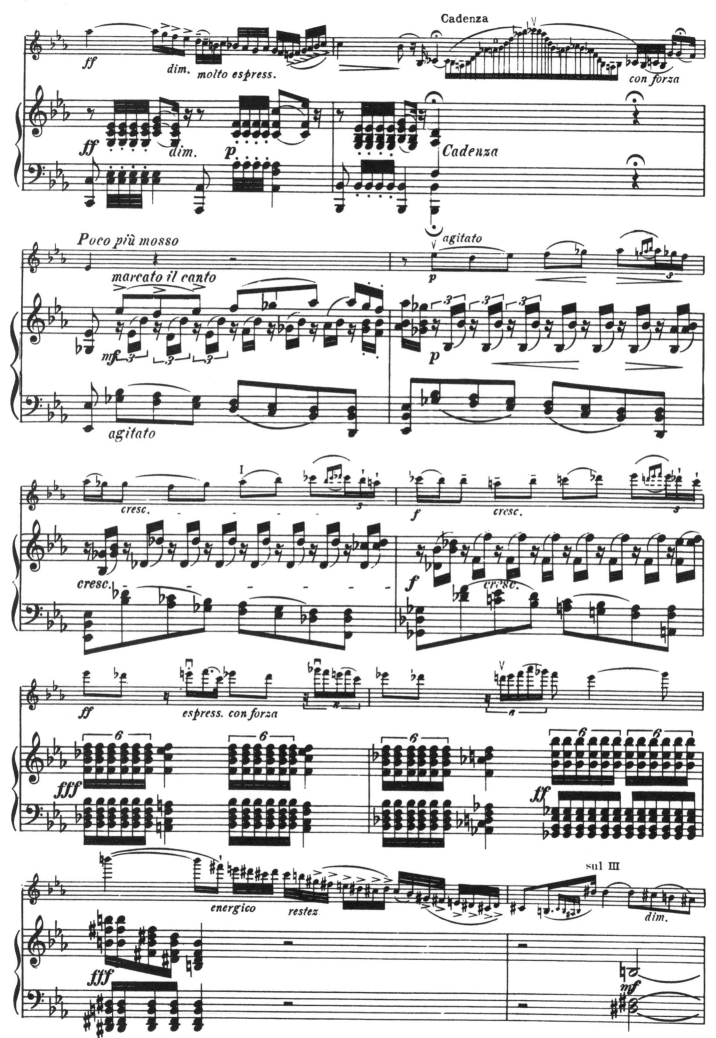

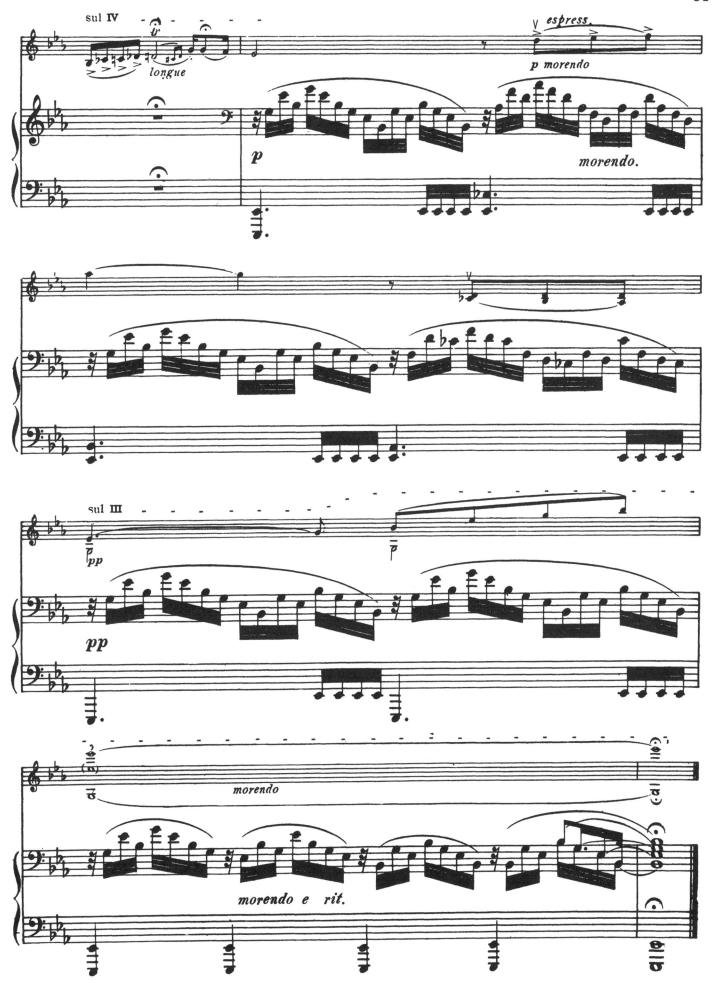

Mazurka

Edited by P. Mittell

Henri Wieniawski, Op. 19, No. 1

Serenade

Arranged by Hans Sitt
Edited by Paul T. Miersch

Franz Schubert

48615